Octopuses and Squid

Tori Miller

PowerKiDS
press

New York

For Tyler

Published in 2009 by The Rosen Publishing Group, Inc.
29 East 21st Street, New York, NY 10010

First Edition

Editor: Joanne Randolph
Book Design: Greg Tucker
Photo Researcher: Jessica Gerweck

Photo Credits: Cover © Reinhard Dirscherl/age fotostock; pp. 5, 7, 15 Shutterstock.com; pp. 9, 19 © Brian J. Skerry/Getty Images; p. 11 © Travel Ink/Getty Images; pp. 12–13 © David Fleetham/Getty Images; pp. 17, 21 © Fred Bavendam/Getty Images.

Library of Congress Cataloging-in-Publication Data

Miller, Tori.
  Octopuses and squid / Tori Miller. — 1st ed.
     p. cm. — (Freaky fish)
  Includes index.
  ISBN 978-1-4358-2757-8 (library binding) — ISBN 978-1-4358-3174-2 (pbk.)
ISBN 978-1-4358-3180-3 (6-pack)
  1. Octopuses—Juvenile literature. 2. Squids—Juvenile literature. I. Title.
  QL430.3.O2M55 2009
  594'.56—dc22
                                        2008035084

Manufactured in the United States of America

Contents

Monsters of the Deep

There are many stories about sea monsters. Often, these monsters are very large with many arms. In the stories, they pull ships under water and eat everyone on board! Many of these stories are likely based on octopuses and squid. Thankfully, real octopuses and squid do not sink ships or eat people!

You are bigger than most squid and octopuses. Most octopuses and squid are about 3 feet (1 m) long. They do not often attack, or try to hurt, people unless they think they are in danger. Even though they look scary, octopuses and squid are likely more afraid of people than we are of them.

This squid is one freaky-looking sea animal. Squid and octopuses can be tiny or they can grow to be the huge animals that scared sailors into telling stories of sea monsters.

What Is the Same?

What would your body be like if you did not have any bones? Octopuses and squid are both **cephalopods** and are part of the **mollusk** family. This means that they have soft bodies and no bones! Octopuses and squid both have **mantles**, eight arms, and large eyes. Both animals also have very good eyesight.

Octopuses and squid swim the same way. First they fill their bodies with water. Then they push the water out through a narrow tube, or strawlike part, called a **siphon**. As the water flows out, it pushes the squid or the octopus forward. Octopuses and squid can swim in any direction.

This is a squid. Like the octopus, the squid has lots of arms, large eyes, and swims by pushing water out of its body.

What Is Different?

Though octopuses and squid belong to the same family, they have many differences. An octopus's body is like a bag. It is soft and does not have a shell. A squid has a shell, called a pen, under its skin. The pen makes a squid less soft than an octopus. A squid cannot fit itself into a small space, as an octopus can, either. A squid also has two long **tentacles** used in feeding, while an octopus does not.

Both squid and octopuses can be very small. However, the giant squid is about twice as long as the largest octopus.

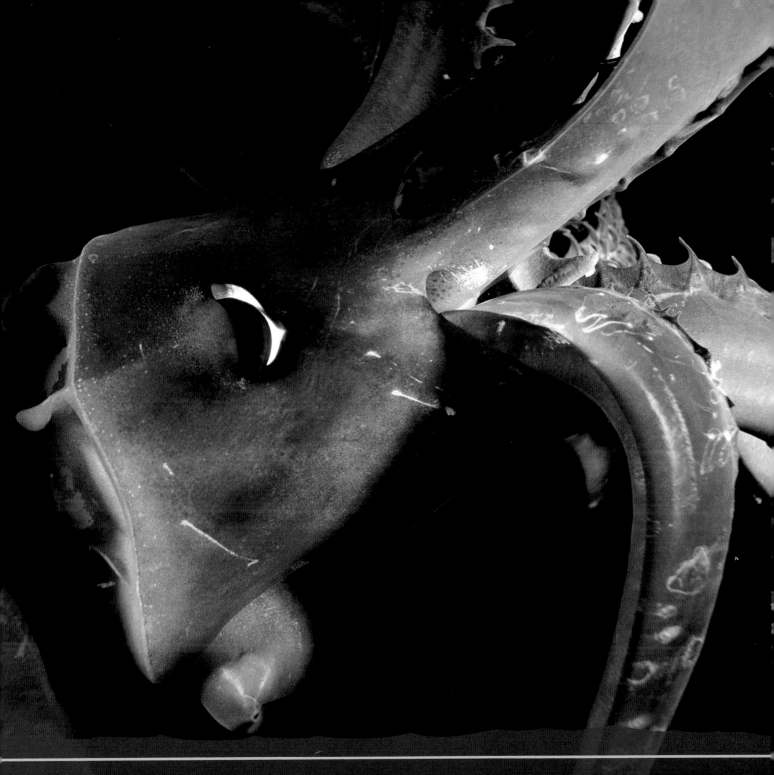

A giant squid, like the one shown here, can be up to 60 feet (18 m) long. That is almost as long as a school bus!

They Are Everywhere!

There are more different species, or kinds, of squid than there are of octopuses. There are about 350 different species of squid and only about 150 different species of octopus.

Squid can be found in all the oceans of the world, even where it is very cold. They can live in very deep water or in water that is not deep. They are fast swimmers. Some kinds of squid can reach speeds of 25 miles per hour (40 km/h). They also sometimes swim in large schools.

Octopuses live in all oceans, except the coldest ones. Octopuses live alone and spend most of their lives hiding in rock dens.

The blue-ringed octopus lives in the Pacific Ocean, from Japan to Australia. It is a small octopus, but its bite makes it one of the world's deadliest sea creatures.

Octopuses and Squid: Freaky Facts

- Octopuses live for only a few years.

- The blue-ringed octopus, which lives in the Pacific Ocean, has **poison** strong enough to kill people.

- The eye of a giant squid can be larger than a person's head.

- Some squid that live in deep water can produce light with their bodies.

- A female octopus eats very little while caring for her eggs. This can last for a period of several months.

- Baby octopuses are only about ¼ inch (6 mm) long.

- Octopuses and squid have three hearts.

°Octopuses and squid have a metal called copper in their blood. The copper makes their blood blue!

°If an octopus loses an arm in a fight, it will grow another one.

°An octopus will change color when it is scared.

13

Arms, Tentacles, and Suckers

Both octopuses and squid have eight arms. There are rows of **suction cups** along each arm. The suction cups help these cephalopods hold on to rocks when they are moving. They also use their suckers to catch and hold prey, or the animals they hunt for food.

Squid have two long tentacles, in addition to their arms. The tentacles have club-shaped tips that are covered with suction cups. Squid use their tentacles to catch food.

Can you imagine tasting things with your arms? An octopus does that! An octopus has taste **receptors** all over its suction cups.

The round white shapes on this octopus's arm are suction cups. These suction cups let octopuses and squid hold on to objects, such as rocks or food, very tightly.

Catching Prey

Octopuses and squid eat shrimp, **crustaceans**, fish, and even other mollusks and cephalopods! Octopuses hunt near rocks and reefs, or underwater hills made of the bodies of small sea animals. An octopus may attack its prey with its whole body. It can also use its long arms to reach into openings and pull out its prey. An octopus poisons its prey before eating it.

Squid hunt in the open ocean. A squid uses its long tentacles to catch its prey. Then it will hold the prey with its arms and eat it. Both squid and octopuses have hard beaks, or birdlike mouthparts, that they use to break shells and tear apart food.

When an octopus spreads its arms out, there is skin in between its arms. It uses this skin like a fishing net, with help from its suckers, to catch its food.

Escaping Enemies

The soft bodies of squid and octopuses make them a yummy dinner for **predators**. Big fish, seals, whales, eels, and some birds eat octopuses and squid. People eat octopuses and squid, too. Have you ever eaten calamari? That is squid!

Octopuses and squid have many ways to keep from being eaten. They can hide from predators by changing colors to match the plants, rocks, and sand around them. They can send out a dark cloud of ink to confuse their enemies while they swim away. Octopuses can hide in very small spaces. Squid can swim quickly and even jump out of the water to escape a predator!

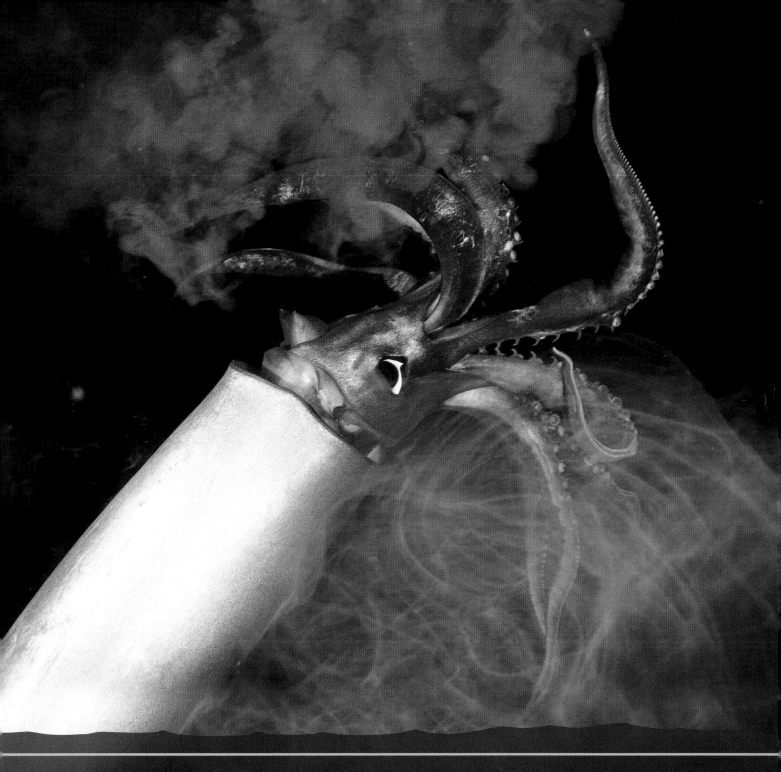

This squid has just released a cloud of ink. Squid and octopuses can control the shape of the ink

Thousands of Eggs

Octopuses and squid change colors to draw a **mate** to them. Once mating happens, a female octopus or squid may lay thousands of eggs at one time.

Many squid come to one place to mate. Squid eggs are fixed to rocks or the ocean floor. Squid die soon after they mate.

Octopuses lay their eggs in dens. An octopus takes good care of her eggs. She guards them and keeps them clean. She does not leave the den, even to eat. Soon after the eggs hatch, or break open, the mother octopus dies. The babies must take care of themselves.

Each Pacific giant octopus egg and newborn octopus seen here is about the size of a grain of rice. If the tiny babies do not get eaten, these octopuses can grow to be 16 feet (5 m) long.

Smart Mollusks?

Octopuses and squid have large brains. Scientists have discovered that squid and octopuses are very smart, at least among mollusks! They can recognize different **textures**. They can also be trained to recognize different shapes. Some octopuses can even figure out how to get things out of a sealed jar. Can you imagine seeing an octopus open a pickle jar?

Octopuses also have good memories, meaning they remember things that happened in the past. Scientists have found that octopuses can remember something that happened several weeks earlier. If an octopus went to school, it would be good at taking quizzes!

Glossary

cephalopods (SEH-fuh-luh-podz) Mollusks that have soft bodies and many arms with suckers. They generally can also shoot ink and have no outer shells. Octopuses, squid, and cuttlefish are cephalopods.

crustaceans (krus-TAY-shunz) Animals that have no backbones, have hard shells and other body parts, and live mostly in water.

mantles (MAN-tulz) Bags of skin and other tissue around the insides of mollusks, such as cephalopods.

mate (MAYT) An animal with which another animal comes together to make babies.

mollusk (MAH-lusk) An animal without a backbone and with a soft body and, often, a shell.

poison (POY-zun) Matter made by an animal's body that causes pain or death.

predators (PREH-duh-terz) Animals that kill other animals for food.

receptors (rih-SEP-terz) Special cells that take in messages.

siphon (SY-fun) A tube-shaped organ, or part, used for spraying out water.

suction cups (SUK-shun KUPS) Cup-shaped disks that animals use to hold on to or stick to things.

tentacles (TEN-tih-kulz) Long, thin growths on animals that are used to touch, hold, or move.

textures (TEKS-churz) The feeling of things when you touch them.

Index

Web Sites

Due to the changing nature of Internet links, PowerKids Press has developed an online list of Web sites related to the subject of this book. This site is updated regularly. Please use this link to access the list:
www.powerkidslinks.com/ffish/octopus/